Hula O Makee*

* **Hula,** which means *dancing* in the Hawaiian language, is an ancient ceremonial dance. The movements of the dancers tell a story or describe the island scenery. The dance is graceful, with swaying body movements and expressive motions of arms, hands and fingers.

   Hula O Makee is a nautical dance named after James Makee, a sea captain.

Paahana (hula)*

* **Paahana** means *energetic workers*. This hula melody is a rustic dance describing the work of people on a farm.

Lei Day

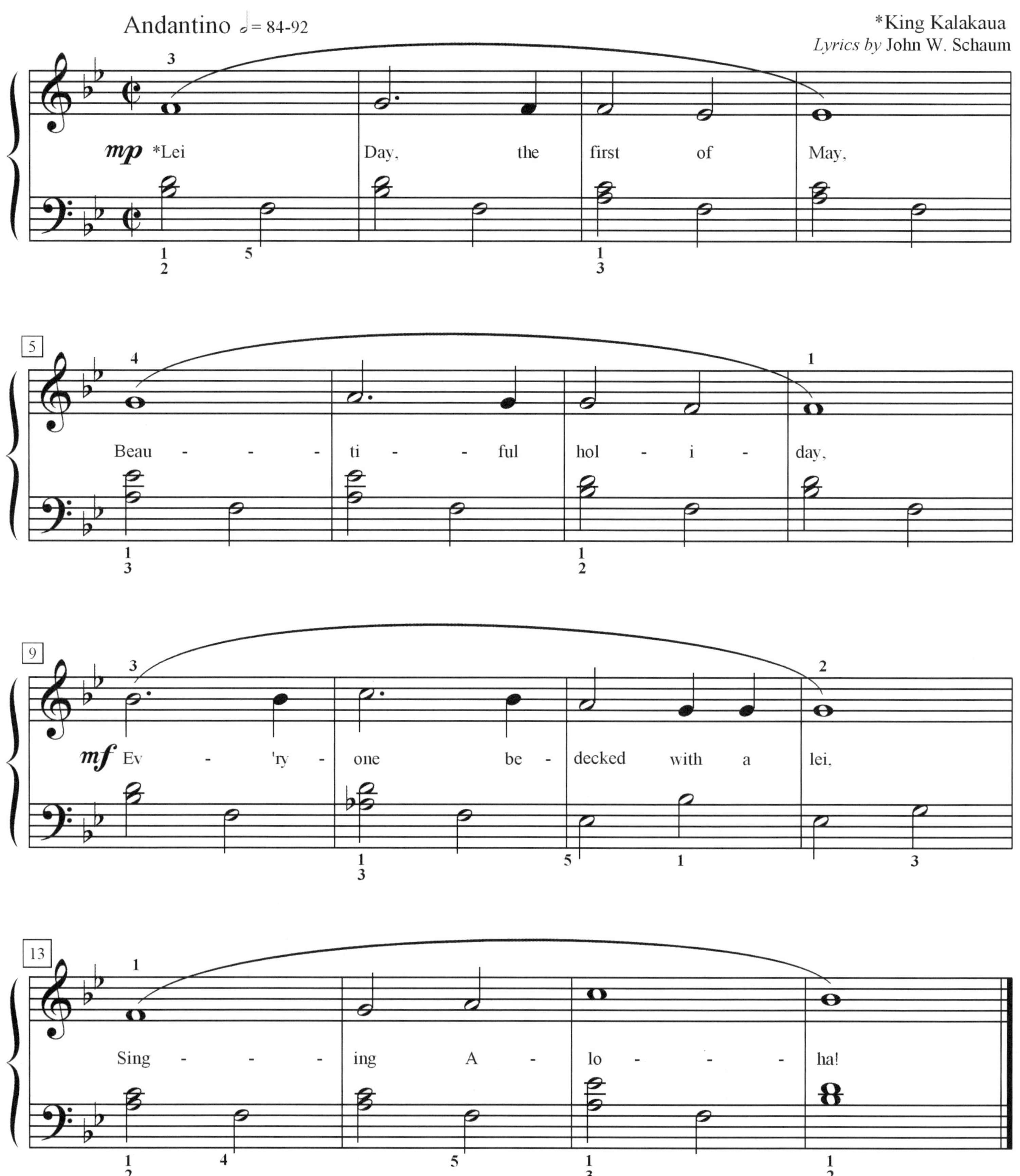

* A *lei* is a garland worn around the neck, usually made of fresh flowers strung together. It may also be made of feathers, shells, seeds, pieces of coral, or ivory. Native Hawaiians wear leis on special occasions. A lei is the symbol of Hawaii's welcome and hospitality.

King David Kalakaua was King of Hawaii from 1874 to 1891. During his reign, the popularity of native Hawaiian customs and music was revived.

Hawaai Ponoi*

* This is the official state song of Hawaii. It was composed by King Kalakaua and made Hawaii's national anthem in 1876 when Hawaii was a Kingdom. After Hawaii became the 50th state in 1959, *Hawaii Ponoi,* meaning "Hawaii's Own [people]," became the state song in 1967.

Waipio*

* *Waipio* is a scenic green valley between steep mountains with many waterfalls. *Waipio* means "curved water" (waterfall). It is sometimes called the "Valley of the Kings" because many of the early Hawaiian kings once lived there. The valley is on the island of Hawaii, the largest of the Hawaiian islands.

At the Luau*

Traditional
Lyrics by John W. Schaum

* A ***Luau*** (LOO-ow) is a Hawaiian outdoor feast featuring roast pork cooked in a pit, along with many other foods native to Hawaii. Luaus often include colorful entertainment with native dancing and singing.

   Luau literally means the leaf of the tropical *taro* plant. The large taro leaves are used in cooking many of the foods served at a luau. The root of the taro plant is used in making *poi*, a basic food similar to cooked oatmeal in texture.

Aloha Oe

* Queen Liluokalani (lee-lee-OO-oh-kah-LAH-nee) was the last reigning monarch of Hawaii before it became a territory of the United States. The queen reigned from 1891-1893. She was a brilliant woman and a talented composer.